# TRAVELS WITH SPOT

## ROME TO BARCELONA

BY

PARKER G. EMERSON

COVER DESIGN BY

CHERYL J.E. ADAMS

TRAVELS WITH SPOT:

ROME TO BARCELONA

COVER ART BY CHERYL J.E. ADAMS

ALL PHOTOGRAPHS BY PARKER G. EMERSON

HARDCOVER ISBN = 978-1-969439-00-1
PAPERBACK ISBN = 978-1-969439-01-8
E-BOOK ISBN = 978-1-969439-02-5
AUDIOBOOK ISBN = 978-1-969439-03-2

LIBRARY OF CONGRESS CONTROL NUMBER:
2025918251

ALSO BY PARKER G. EMERSON

TRAVELS WITH SPOT: Paris to Zürich

The Public Administrator's Companion: A Practical
Guide 2nd edition

# DEDICATION

The TRAVELS WITH SPOT books are dedicated to my supportive and patient wife, Sandra; to all who long to travel and cannot but want to know what it's like to be where I've been; and to those who want to know what to expect beyond what guidebooks provide.

# Table of Contents

# ACKNOWLEDGEMENTS

This book would not have been possible without the constant support and encouragement of my wonderful wife, Sandra, who often wonders where she was when she reads my stories of our adventures. A special thank you to Mary Hruby for beta-reading the draft and making several inciteful suggestions; virgin eyes are always useful. I also thank the folks at Parker Publishers, LLC, who stepped up to the plate and facilitated publishing this book in only four months from receiving my inquiry; thank you, Jay Davis and Arthur Blair.

# ABOUT THE AUTHOR

Parker has traveled throughout the United States, Europe, and parts of Africa, Mexico, and South Korea beginning with an unguided trip to Europe in 1973. At that time he spoke a little German, enough French to get into serious trouble, and used Frommer's *EUROPE ON $5 A DAY* to find lodgings, restaurants, sights to see, and to navigate around the cities by the book-size maps in the book. He was also the navigation center supervisor on the nuclear missile submarine *USS SIMON BOLIVAR* (SSBN 641) for eight years and fifteen deployments deterring global thermonuclear war. He completed his B.S. in business administration at Old Dominion University in Norfolk, VA, while still on active duty. After leaving the US Navy, he moved to California where he worked in the aerospace industry and simultaneously earned his MBA from the University of Southern California. Mr. Emerson has held senior management positions and has started and sold several companies. He co-authored *The Public Administrator's Companion: A Practical Guide 2nd edition* as well writes the *TRAVELS WITH SPOT* series of travel stories.

Now retired, he and his wife Sandra enjoy traveling, mostly on guided tours having learned valuable lessons from their 1973 adventures in Europe, and writing about their adventures.

# 1 – GETTING TO ROME

We have long wanted to see Rome, Florence, and Barcelona for their art and history. This is the plan: at 8:00 a.m. fly from Ontario International Airport in California, arrive in Dallas/Fort Worth at 12:59 that afternoon, then continue to Rome, arriving at 8:00 the next morning and board the *Viking Sky* at 11:30 in time to take the bus tour through Rome before the ship leaves at 10:00 p.m. for Florence.

It's a nice plan.

That is not what happens.

Sandra and I arrive at Ontario International Airport two hours early, like we're supposed to. We check our bags through to Rome, then endure the TSA partial stripping, bin-loading, scanning, bin discovery, and dressing exercise. TSA is not too bad this morning because it's early and the agents are not yet surly from dealing with passengers who still have not figured out that neither a 32-ounce bottle of water nor a loaded pistol are allowed through the checkpoint. Our gate for American flight 1534 is only fifty feet away. We wait patiently, occasionally walking around and stopping at the opening stores when our bottoms get numb from the hard seats in the gate area.

Around 8:10 a.m. the plane pulls in, people get off from the early flight from Salt Lake City, and we wait for boarding to begin. Our scheduled departure time comes, and it goes.

There is some activity behind the counter at the gate, but no boarding. At 8:30 they announce, "A baggage truck may have hit the plane, so we must wait until maintenance can inspect the plane to check for any damage. We would like to apologize for the delay."

They would like to apologize, but they do not actually apologize.

Forty-five minutes later, another announcement. "We're still waiting for the inspectors to arrive to check the plane. Again, we would like to apologize for the delay. We'll start boarding as soon as they clear the plane for flight."

I'm starting to get concerned since we originally had only 90 minutes to change planes in Dallas/Fort Worth, and we've already used up 75 of them. I go and speak with the gate agent.

"My wife and I MUST be in Rome early tomorrow to catch our ship. Here are our boarding passes. Is there another flight that will get us there in time? It doesn't look like we'll be able to make the connection in Dallas unless we take off in the next fifteen minutes and arrive at the gate right beside the flight to Rome, which doesn't seem likely."

"Let me see what we can do," she replies and starts typing at her terminal.

"Our ship leaves Rome at 8:00 pm tomorrow, so we need to arrive no later than 6:00 pm to get to the ship," I tell her.

"Uh, huh."

She doesn't seem to understand our timing concerns and continues typing, points at the screen, nods her head, and smiles as she prints out two new ticket sets for Sandra and me.

"I've rebooked your flights for you from LAX to Heathrow to Rome. Here you go."

"Thanks, but how are we supposed to get to LAX from here? It's 57 miles away."

"Oh. Just a moment. I'll get you a voucher for a taxi to LAX. No charge to you. Just bring it to the taxi stand outside and they'll take you."

"OK. We've checked our bags through to Rome. Will they still make it there?"

"Wait just a minute and we'll get your bags off this plane to take with you to LAX."

"Thank you very much."

In about five minutes our bags are delivered to us. This may be the shortest time it has taken for us to get our checked bags. We head out to the taxi stand, hand the driver the voucher, load our bags and us, and we're off to LAX.

While we are en route, I call the Viking Travel Coordinator to let them know our flights have changed so they can meet us at the airport in Rome and take us to the ship.

"Hi. Our original flight from Ontario got delayed so we won't be able to take the flights you've scheduled for us. American Airlines rebooked us on different flights, and we're currently on our way from Ontario International Airport to LAX. Our new tickets are go from LAX to Heathrow to Rome" I give her the exact flight information.

She repeats the flight information I gave her, pauses, and says, "Well, that won't work. That flight from Heathrow won't arrive in Rome until 10:40 pm and the ship sails at 10:00. Let's see what we can do."

As she works her magic, I wonder what we would have done if we did not have cell phones with the ability to call from anywhere, including a taxi between airports.

"Here are the flights you'll need: LAX to Madrid to Rome on Iberia Airline," and she reads the details. "You'll have two hours to make the connection in Madrid."

"That's great. How do I get the tickets the airline gave me changed to the ones I need?"

"When you get to LAX, go to the American ticket counter and tell them the flights you will need."

I ask her to repeat the flight information so I can write it down, then thank her, hang up, and take a deep breath.

"Well, this is shaping up to be more of an adventure than we thought it would be," I say to Sandra as we ride the freeways for an hour and a half between airports.

Arriving at LAX, we head to the American Airlines ticket counter with our bags. I approach an open ticket agent.

"Hi. Can you please help us? We were scheduled for a flight from Ontario, but a baggage truck dented the plane which delayed the flight so we wouldn't be able to make our connections to Rome. The gate agent rebooked us on these flights."

I hand her the tickets and continue. "But these won't get us into Rome until after our ship has sailed, literally. The ticketing agent at the cruise line says we need these flights instead." I hand her my notebook with the flights through Madrid.

"Why did you book these flights through Heathrow if they wouldn't get you to Rome in time?" she asks.

"Actually, I didn't. The gate agent in Ontario booked them."

"Well, there'll be a change fee to issue new tickets."

"What? I didn't select these flights, your gate agent in Ontario did."

"But now you want different flights."

The conversation is rapidly heading into a rabbit hole with Alice, so I call the Viking Travel Coordinator again and ask her to speak directly with the airline agent and work things out. It takes them twenty minutes or so to resolve the tickets and payments (we don't have to pay for the change).

We are given new boarding passes but have to go to the Iberia Airlines counter to check our bags through to Rome.

There is no one at the Iberia counter. Even the light is off. The flight is not due to depart until 5:55 p.m. and it's only 11:30 a.m.

At 1:00 the light above the Iberia counter lights up, but no one is at the counter.  People start lining up and we join the line weaving through the serpentine barriers to face an empty counter. People go to get drinks and sandwiches or just to get some exercise or sit for a while and then return to the line. No one from the airline seems to be in a rush.

An hour and a quarter later a couple of staff arrive behind the counter and start processing the people in line. We check our bags through to Rome and head to TSA for our second screening of the morning. Oh joy. I can't wait to take off my shoes and belt again, hoping my pants stay up.

My pants do stay up, but when I collect my several bins of shoes, jacket, belt, wallet, and watch, I notice that the bin with my computer has been set to one side behind a Plexiglass shield. This does not bode well. The agent who set it aside leaves the area. Is he taking a break? Getting coffee? Getting a supervisor? Going home? And then the bin is completely ignored. Agents walk past it without a glance. I guess that since they didn't put it there, they won't have to do anything with it.

I hang around the end of the security area waiting for someone to get to my bin and give me my computer. An agent who has been flitting around the area approaches me, waving her hands in a "shoo" motion.

"Go on. Move along."

"But my bag is still there." I point to it behind the Plexiglas.

"We'll get to it. Just go over there and sit down."

"But it's been there for ten minutes, and no one has touched it or even looked at it."

"Don't you worry about it. We'll get to it. Just wait."

"How long do you think it will be? I do have a flight to catch."

"When we get to it, we get to it. Now get away from here."

She is clearly getting irritated at me, and I resist the urge to reciprocate, knowing that it would only extend an already slow process and possibly make it even worse. I would really like to avoid a strip search.

Ten minutes later a newly arrived agent puts the bin on a counter, motions for me to come over but to stand five feet away, puts on latex gloves with a great show, and dumps everything out of the computer bag beside the computer before poking around through the papers, cables, pens, sleep mask, ear plugs, charger, and collapsable umbrella.

He looks at me, says, "OK," and walks away.

"Can I take my stuff now?" I ask.

"Yeah."

I carefully pack everything back into the computer bag in the appropriate pockets so I can find them later.

TSA should put a sign up over their stations: "YOUR VACATION MEMORIES START HERE."

At 3:20 Sandra and I find the gate for our flight. Just as we sit down, we hear an announcement, "Delta Flight 8553 is in final boarding for Rome. Final call for Delta Flight 8553 direct to Rome." Now why didn't they book us on that flight? Instead, we have to wait another two and a half hours and change planes in Madrid. All because a baggage truck driver bumped into our plane.

The flights to Madrid and then to Rome are on time and quite comfortable. The food is good and the attendants attentive. Nothing particularly remarkable except the flights are completely unremarkable – exactly what we desire for air travel.

We arrive at Fiumicino "Leonardo da Vinci" International Airport servicing Rome at 6:50 pm on July 23, breeze through customs, claim our bags, meet our Viking driver, and wait for some more people who are arriving on a later flight. The airport is west of Rome near the coast and our ship is in Civitavecchia Port about forty-one miles away. We don't get to see any of Rome. With the arrival of several more people, we board the bus for the 45-minute drive to the *Viking Sky*. At 9:30 pm (21:30 European time) we are in our stateroom, coincidentally number 2130, and Sonny, our steward, shows us where everything is and how to use our boarding card to make the lights work. It has been a long day, and Sandra and I are happy to unpack and fall into bed. We are sound asleep when the ship sets sail a half hour later.

# 2 - FLORENCE

We begin our day with breakfast in *The Restaurant,* the arresting but clear name for the main restaurant, as the ship sails towards Livorno, the port serving the Florence area. Coffee, bagel with cream cheese, an omelet with sauteed onions and diced ham for Sandra; scrambled eggs, hardboiled eggs, cranberry juice, blueberries with yogurt, and an English muffin for me. A decent breakfast sets us up for a good day. Experience tells us that we will need the protein and the carbohydrates.

Returning to our stateroom, Sonny, the steward, knocks on the door and comes in with a special cake from the ship for our 50$^{th}$ wedding anniversary. We thank Sonny and put the cake in the small refrigerator to save it for the actual anniversary which will be in five days. At 9:00 a.m. the ship docks near a large cruise ship with 4,000 or more passengers, which makes our 960-passenger ship look like a toy.

At 9:30 we board a bus that takes us into Firenze (Florence to English-speakers) for the "Fiat 500 Experience." This will involve driving in the countryside around Firenze in the namesake car, followed by some time on our own in the city.

## THE FIAT 500 EXPERIENCE

Arriving in Firenze, we meet Andrea who leads us and four others from the cruise to a fleet of three Fiat 500 vehicles and their drivers for our experience. These are small vehicles; smaller than the classic VW 'bug' but similar in shape. It is powered by a 479-CC — hence the optimistic name Fiat 500 — two-cylinder engine generating 13 horsepower and a three-speed manual transmission. While there are more modern Fiat 500's with larger engines, these are classic early models. This is a car built for Sandra's nearly 5-foot-tall frame, with its roof just below her shoulders. However, it only reaches 6-foot-tall Andrea's elbows. Its canvas sunroof is retracted so his head does not cause it to bulge. The model we will be in is a Nuova 500, and Andrea proudly wears a T-shirt with pictures of the two engineers who designed the car. FIAT, by the way, stands for Fabbrica Italiana di Automobili Torino.

It's obvious that Sandra and I cannot both fit in the back seat, so Sandra flips the driver's seat forward and wedges herself in while Andrea slides the passenger seat to its farthest-back position for me. Andrea folds himself into the driver's seat and I carefully maneuver myself into the car, grasping the door and roof for support. Both his and my knees stick up like we are sitting in kiddie chairs, and our hair would brush the sunroof if it were not retracted.

We both instinctively crouch forward, careful not to hit the edge of the roof opening. I cannot see how Sandra is faring in the back, but she says she's fine. "This is just my size." Andrea is very proud of his Fiat, smiling broadly as he starts it. A light cloud of smoke and burnt gasoline fumes envelop us, but they die away as we get in motion.

**Figure 1 Andrea and Sandra beside the Fiat 500**

We follow one of the other Fiats, are out of the city in only a minute or two, and putter on a grand tour through the countryside. The car's size is well suited to the narrow roads and sharp turns. We frequently pull far to the side, brushing vegetation, to let other cars pass in either direction. Andrea shifts into first gear to climb several hills, and I ask him to leave more space between us and the lead car so its exhaust can dissipate before it wafts in our windows. There are a couple of times when I wonder if I should get out so the fully loaded car can make it; but, like the little engine that could, it successfully mounts every hill.

Olive trees and grapevines, two essentials for life in Italy, cover every hillside. The pleasant light scent of their leaves contrasts with the occasional whiff of gasoline fumes. Once grand but still well-maintained estate houses crown the highest hills, and the views evoke images of Renaissance Italian landscapes. Rolling hills, vineyards, olive trees, narrow roads to hilltop villas lined with spires of cypress trees, and blue skies with friendly puffy white clouds complete the idyllic image.

After ninety minutes or so, we stop at a restaurant overlooking Firenze. We take several minutes to extricate ourselves from the car; it really is compact. Andrea leads us through marble halls to tables in the shade where glasses of water await. The people from the other two Fiats have already been seated. A waitress takes our orders for refreshments which are included as part of the tour. Sandra orders a strawberry and chocolate gelato while I opt for crème and chocolate.Wine is extra but completes the ambiance. This is Italy, after all. What would you drink besides wine or Prosecco? At the edge of the patio overlooking the city is a bronze replica of Michaelangelo's *David*. The view is the classic postcard: red tile roofs, crème walls, and Brunelleschi's red dome on the cathedral towering above everything else.

Our next stop is at the Abbazia San Miniato al Monte, a Benedictine abbey founded in 1018 which, as its name states, sits on a hill high above the city[1]. The legend is that Miniato was a third century Armenian soldier who wanted to testify to his faith in Christ until he was martyred. There were several but ineffective attempts to kill him, including hanging, poisoning, and being dragged behind a cart. But he survived until finally Roman soldiers under emperor Decius decapitated him on the banks of the river Arno in 250 AD. Not willing to die ignominiously by the river, which was also the city sewer, Miniato picked up his own head and climbed the hill to where the abbey now stands before he died and was buried there. His martyrdom didn't make a great impression at the time; there were of lots of Christians being killed in the third century. Five hundred years later his story was revived, and a church was finally built in his honor on the site. Unfortunately, it fell into

---

[1] See https://sanminiatoalmonte-it.translate.goog/abbazia-di-san-miniato/?_x_tr_sl=it&_x_tr_tl=en&_x_tr_hl=en&_x_tr_pto=sc

disrepair over the next three hundred years until the Florentine bishop Ildebrando razed the old building and started the current Romanesque Basilica in 1018 CE.

The facade is marvelous with three double copper-green doors, intricate patterns of grey on white marble, a mosaic of Christ sitting on a throne holding a book in his left hand and extending a blessing with his right. A fledged eagle stands atop the steeple at the peak of the roof. The limestone carvings of animal heads under the eaves and decorative patterns have survived well. I'm sure the interior is dazzling, but it is closed, and we are left to ponder the view of the city and one of the oldest Christian cemeteries in Florence. The many plots with elaborate statuary and lids of stone or bronze include the names of multiple burials, and each plot has several flower vases. Tending and visiting these graves requires stamina, since there are fifty or so steps up to the cemetery from the road below and another fifty or so down from the abbey courtyard above.

Returning to the city by a circuitous route through more olive groves and vineyards, we bid *ciao* to Andrea and the Fiats and roam the shops along the street leading to the small park where our bus will meet us. It's hot (over 100F), so we slink through the shadows and dally in those shops with air conditioning. Sandra buys a belt and a few leather keychains while I watch a craftsman deboss[2] gold-leaf initials into a leather handbag for a customer. I always enjoy watching artisans working at their crafts, selecting the proper tools, manipulating the objects, and ensuring that the finished product is as fine as they can make it. It's the opposite of mass production.

We stop in the Piazza di Santa Croce with the Church of Santa Croce[3] at one end and a statue in front dated 1865 labeled "A. Dante Alighieri L'Italia." This guy, who wrote The Divine Comedy, is dressed as a Roman emperor, complete with imperial toga, an eagle looking admiringly up at him, and a crown of laurels on his head as he scowls at us mere mortals below.

The church façade, like the Abbazia San Miniato al Monte, is white marble with grey inlay patterns and well-preserved carvings. In a niche above the center door is a statue of what appears to be a woman holding a book; it's not clear to me if this is Mary or, given the adoration Florentines accorded Dante, if this might be his beloved Beatrice. It's still hot and the building is closed for some restoration work, so we turn to go to the park where we will meet the bus.

---

[2] Debossing is when letters or images are pressed into the material. Embossing is when the letters or images are raised from the surface of the material.

[3] See https://www.santacroceopera.it/en/

Above us, an apartment facing the piazza displays European Union and Italian flags above a banner proclaiming "Libertà Patrick Zaky" and a drawing of a bespectacled man with tousled hair, a beard, and a moustache. I'm intrigued. What's this all about? It turns out that he is a Coptic Egyptian who's pursuing a master's degree in Women and Gender Studies at the University of Bologna and advocating for the Egyptian Initiative of Personal Rights. The Egyptian government arrested and held him in Cairo in 2020 (two years ago) without trial. He became a *cause célèbres* in Italy which granted him Italian citizenship in 2021 by a special act of Parliament to help get him released, which he was in December 2021, but the charges against him have not been dropped by Egypt.[4]

The bus picks us up for the forty-five-minute drive back to the ship. I'm sorry, but from a distance, the Viking Sky does look like a toy next to the large cruise ship.

---

[4] He was eventually found guilty of the charges of, effectively, embarrassing the state, and was immediately pardoned by the Egyptian president in 2023

# 3 – SMALL TOWNS

Today we visit a couple of the hamlets and small towns North and West of Florence to get a feel for rural Italy. Too often tours take us to only the large cities and big tourist spots preventing us from experiencing what I call "the real places" where people live and work.

## VINCI

After another fine breakfast of eggs, blueberries, yogurt, coffee, and juice, we're off to the hamlet of Vinci, home to a famous person, to see the Museo Leonardiano Vinci.[5] Our guide on this trip is Lucia Galli whose English is excellent and unaccented except when saying Italian words, which is appropriate. She introduces us to the subject of the museum.

"Leonardo was simultaneously a sculptor, a painter, an architect, an engineer, a polymath, a naturalist, an anatomist, a philosopher, and an inventor. He was generally not known as Leonardo *da Vinci* during his lifetime. That came much later. At birth, his name was simply *Leonardo*. Most people at the time had only one name, although occasionally they also used their father's name to distinguish themselves from others with the same

---

[5] Website https://www.museoleonardiano.it

name. This was true not only in Tuscany and Italy, but also throughout most of Europe. In Leonardo's case he was also known as *Leonardo di ser Piero* or 'Leonardo of Sir Piero.' When he traveled outside the Republic of Florence, he usually referred to himself as *Leonardo the Florentine*. He might properly be known as *Leonardo da Anchiano* since that was the nearby hamlet in which he was born. However, his father's family were important in the nearby slightly larger hamlet of Vinci, so he was sometimes called *Leonardo da Vinci* by others, but probably not in his presence.

"The first syllable of his name, as you may have guessed from my pronunciation, is properly pronounced 'Lay-' and the accent is on the third syllable, which is drawn out slightly, resulting in 'Lay-o-nar-do.' In the art world, he is simply known as Leonardo, as in 'The Mona Lisa is by Leonardo'."

The museum is on the Palazzina Uzielli, part of the Castello die Guidi on a hill above Vinci, a rustic town of olive trees, vineyards, and red tiled roofs on crème-colored buildings. The grounds around the museum area are not nice flat square plazas but are quite irregular in both shape and texture covering a very hilly hilltop. The stone plazas are decorated with patterned tiles and sculptures derived from Leonardo's sketches.

A stunning sculpture provides a three-dimensional interpretation of the sketch of a man with outstretched arms and legs touching the corners of a square drawn inside a circle. This "Vitruvian man," standing inside a cube inside a globe framework, illustrates the beauty, balance, and proportions of the ideal man from all angles.

A stainless-steel sculpture with five-sided pyramids extending from each face of a dodecahedron is the centerpiece of another small plaza.

**Figure 2 Dodecahedron sculpture at Museo Leonardiano Vinci**

Adorning a small hillside between buildings are a rough wooden sculpture of a goat grazing and three bronze balls with six long thin spikes extending from their surfaces. I'm not certain what the balls are, but I take them to represent either porcupines or briar seeds which stick aggressively to clothing.

Luccia Galli, the guide, points out, "As you stand on the piazza and look over the countryside, you can see the hills and distant mountains that inspired many of Leonardo's backgrounds. If you look carefully, you'll notice that the farther you look, not only do trees and objects become less clearly defined, they also take on a blue tinge. The farther away, the bluer the tinge, but the shading changes continuously and imperceptibly. Leonardo used this phenomenon in many of his paintings to give a sense of depth to the setting. He pioneered and developed this technique called *sfumato*."

A tower with an observation platform and bells soars from the highest point in the collection of buildings. This is a common feature in Tuscan towns. Lookouts in the towers would scan the surrounding countryside and ring the bells to alert the town of approaching armies or dignitaries' entourages. In the case of approaching armies, townspeople, or at least the Duke's family, would retreat to the protection of the tower while preparing to fend off the enemy. In the case of approaching dignitaries, the town would prepare to properly welcome them.

The first building we enter is the Chiesa di Santa Croce (Church of the Holy Cross) which includes the baptistry where Leonardo was baptized. The nave is cool, a happy respite from the heat outside, and dimly lit by a single narrow stained-glass window behind the rough-hewn wood altar and six small arched windows twenty feet above the floor. Four columns support Romanesque arches on either side of the nave, separating it from the ambulatory. Ten simple wood pews with kneeling benches and room for only three people abreast on each side of the central aisle essentially complete the interior of this charming rustic church serving the small hamlet.

The baptistry is a semi-circular alcove just inside the entrance. The bronze lid of the round font takes two people and a great deal of effort to tilt open on its hinge. A wonderful metal sculpture of the Last Supper by Cecco Bonanotte seemingly floats in midair from the wall nearby. I find this an interesting juxtaposition: baptism signifying the beginning of life and the Last Supper portending the end of temporal life but the beginning of eternal life.

We carefully make our way over the uneven and steep cobbles from the church to the museum. Once inside, we are surrounded by reconstructions of equipment designed by Leonardo. They're fascinating. It's not known how many of the engineering devices Leonardo ever actually built. Many of his inventive drawings are for military applications. This makes sense since he sold his talents to the Medicis and others as a designer of city defenses, not as a painter or sculptor. Some, like a man-powered battle tank with a cut-out to show its inner workings, are scale models. A full-size ten-barrel wheeled cannon firing a fusillade of one-inch balls over a wide swath would be devastating to a charging line of infantry. A wheeled canon with a vertical aiming scale firing a three-inch ball presages long-range cannons with ballistic trajectory calculations. A model of a self-supporting bridge that can be quickly deployed by troops in the field illustrated his understanding of practical military needs beyond flashy weaponry.

Many sketches and models are for domestic devices, such as one to simultaneously spin four threads and wind them on spools. This would have greatly increased the productivity of weavers because making the thread was a very labor-intensive process, usually only one thread and spool at a time.

A full-size rendering of the wood and canvas wing apparatus for man-powered flying covering most of the ceiling of one room is so large it takes Sandra several minutes to figure out what it is. Leonardo was fascinated by flight for most of his life, but the materials available were too heavy and human muscles were simply not strong enough to make human-powered flight possible.

There is a practical industrial tool-making machine to make wooden screws, which were essential to build many of his contraptions. Mechanized manufacturing of standard screws and gears, which are basic parts of most machines, would have revolutionized producing machines of all types. Fascinating stuff. There are also many other mechanical devices built from Leonardo's sketches.

The machines on display are apparently fully functional. The kid in me really wants to turn the cranks and watch them in action, but there are many signs with a hand covered by a red circle with a bar through it, and ropes tied to parts of the mechanisms to keep them from operating. It's sad, but I suppose there are too many kids of all ages who would turn the cranks until they break just to see if they could.

## LUCCA

Our next stop is the town of Lucca about 30 miles from Vinci. The roads and scenes through the small towns and rolling hills are archetypically Tuscan. The country portions of the drive remind me of the movie *Under the Tuscan Sun*. Olive groves and vineyards abound while lanes leading to estate houses are lined with Mediterranean cypress trees standing like tall green flames that seem to cool the whole area. Whitewashed red tile roofed houses dot the countryside and cluster together as we pass through hamlets along the way.

We disembark in a park outside the Porta Sant'Anna, one of the gates to the city where the streets are too narrow for the bus to maneuver. Lucca retains the charms of an idyllic and probably mythic Tuscan city. We enter through the massive stone wall which completely encloses a major section of the city. There are two gates for vehicles and two smaller and narrower gates for pedestrians. The wall saved the city in 1812 when the adjacent Serchio River flooded; all the city gates were closed and sealed keeping most of the city mostly dry.

Lucca was first settled by Ligurians in the third century BCE who called it *Luk* meaning "marsh" and later by Etruscans before the Romans colonized it in 180 BCE. In 56 BCE it hosted the Lucca Conference where Julius Caesar, Pompey, and Crassus met and reaffirmed their political alliance, the First Triumvirate. Over the centuries Lucca has been an independent city-state; a republic; a vassal city ruled at various times by Florence, France, the Duke of Bavaria, the Grand Duchy of Tuscany, Rome, the Lombards, and the Duke of Pisa; before finally becoming an independent city again when the modern Italian state was formed in 1861.

We walk along the Piazzale Guiseppe Verdi to the Via San Paolino and then east toward the Piazza San Michele in the center of Lucca. We stop at the Piazza Cittadella and admire the life-size bronze statue of the opera composer

Giacomo Puccini. He sits in a chair smoking a cigarette with one ankle cast casually on the other knee in front of the Puccini Museum. Placing the statue on a four-foot-high plinth discourages people from sitting on his lap or holding his shoulder while having their picture taken. However, his shoe is shiny from people rubbing it while being photographed.

**Figure 3 Giacomo Puccini statue**

The Piazza Cittadella is intimate, lined with several small opera-named restaurants including Madame Butterfly, Paris Boheme, Bistrot Cucina, Osteria Tosca, and Caffe Manon Lescaut. We browse the menus to consider for an afternoon snack later after touring more of the city.

Two hundred feet down the street we enter the large Piazza San Michele dominated by the San Michele in Foro Roman Catholic basilica. The "in Foro" portion of the name derives from the Roman forum built here before the first church in the eighth century CE. Dedicated to the Archangel Michael, it was rebuilt in the eleventh century under Pope Alexander II.

It's a bit of a platypus in appearance. Built of white marble, the front has a façade soaring half again as tall as the rest of the building. The upper half of the façade contains two rows of fifteen columns topped by two rows of seven columns. These are expensive columns. Each is carved from single blocks of stone, each has a different pattern, each are made from different stone from different quarries as far away as Ur in Mesopotamia (southern Iraq) and Thebes in southern Egypt, and each has its own unique capital. All these columns are topped by a pediment surmounted by a giant statue of the Archangel Michael with bronze wings fledged, an orb with a cross on it in his left hand and a lance in his right. Smaller angels on their own house-like pedestals blowing horns flank him on either side. While there are many columns on all sides and on all levels, they are not structural and the arches are filled in, forming "blind arcades." This gives the impression the arches once graced an airy open space that was later bricked in, making the church look like a solid block of marble that has a nave carved out of its heart. Only three narrow windows on each long side admit light into the interior. The southern transept ends with a square bell tower which is even taller than the façade in front. While there are many ornate and intricate carvings, the lowest are over thirty feet above the ground but are scaled to be seen from eye level. People living in the fourth floor of the buildings facing the church have a nice view of these carvings. My overall impression is that various people paid for various parts of the church and designed their part themselves, with little or no coherent design in mind.

**Figure 4 San Michele in Foro, Lucca, Italy**

We walk south to the Piazza Napoleone where they are taking down stages, lights, and screens from the Lucca Summer Festival which ended yesterday. This is an annual month-long music festival drawing artists and fans from around the world. Some of the performers this year were Ben Harper, John Legend, Celine Dion, Alison Krauss, Paolo Conte, and Kasabian. This is not the only venue for the festival, and we head north to the Piazza dell' Anfiteatro (Amphitheater Square).

Sandra and I enter through a dark alleyway barely wider than the tiny Fiat 500 we rode earlier and emerge into the dazzling sunlight of the large oval plaza which was once the stage of a Roman amphitheater. It was originally similar in design to the Coliseum in Rome with tiers of seats surrounding the central stage, but on a much smaller scale. The plaza is only 270 feet long and 150 wide and the tiers of seats have long since been converted to apartments, several restaurants, a few boutiques, and a small hotel. People crowd under large umbrellas around the perimeter of the plaza shading tables for the restaurants and linger in the shadows of the four- and five-story apartments on the south side. Those eating or nursing a cup of cappuccino are in no particular rush, holding casual conversations with their dining companions and examining the other patrons and passers-by, expressing approval or disappointment with subtle nods, shakes, smiles, or eyerolls. It's a very relaxed atmosphere. No Italian is in a rush until they get into a car and then they seem intent to run you over. Each apartment building is only one or two windows wide facing the piazza, but the rooms expand on the other end. I notice five arched entrances nearly hidden around the piazza and that we entered through the smallest one.

Heading back, we pass by a sand sculpture. The artist has laid a section of red carpet on the ground and sculpted a dog with her four puppies resting in the hot sun gazing forlornly at the passers-by entreating them to leave donations in their water bowl. All the dogs have dark brown balls for eyes, making them very appealing and pleading "Do you want to adopt me? I'm really cute." The artist spritzes them and the carpet with water every few minutes to keep them from drying and crumbling in the hot sun. A five Euro coin seems appropriate for her artistry.

As I walk along the brick and cobblestone roads and sidewalks, it occurs to me that most Europeans are comfortable navigating the uneven surfaces found everywhere. Smooth concrete or asphalt sidewalks or roadways are largely non-existent in the smaller towns and hamlets. I see only American tourists stumbling or tripping over half-inch deviations between stones. Trip-and-fall attorneys must have a meager income in Europe.

We finish our tour back at the Piazza San Michele where we are on our own for a while. Some go for lunch in one of the many cafes and restaurants on the Piazza while others go farther afield to dine or shop. Sandra and I opt for cold sodas from the nearby Bar San Michele and then head slowly back to where we got off the bus. Along the way, we stop at several shops for gifts. Lucca, like many cities in Italy, is very proud of its olive oils, so this seems an appropriate gift for several relatives and friends who enjoy cooking and/or eating. We stop in one shop with a nice selection of olive oils, vinegars, herbs, and hats, but the girl at the counter says that they do not ship items, but "The shop just down the street does." Not wanting to risk having a bottle of olive oil break in our luggage, we thank her, leave a generous tip, and step into La Botique Dei Golosi a few doors away at Via San Paolino No. 80.

Like many Italian shops, this is small and narrow, perhaps eighteen or twenty feet wide and as much as thirty-five feet deep. Cool stucco walls, stone or tile floors, and wood beamed ceiling with fans circulate the air in a very gentle breeze. The owners likely live in the apartment above. This shop is in the middle of the block, so the only windows surround the front door. Various olive oils in bottles ranging from 10 milliliters to 4 liters line one wall, with cruets, salt and pepper boats and shakers, and related items on the opposite wall. The owner greets us from a tiny counter at the far end.

Sandra asks, "Are these local?"

"Si! Si! All of these are from the hills around us. We are very proud of our olive oil which is famous all over Italia."

"Do you ship purchases to the United States?"

"Si! Si! We can package and ship anywhere in the world."

"Great."

We carefully select four 50-milliliter bottles of different olive oils for my sister and three nieces and bring them to the counter. These will be great for salads. I hand my business card to the shopkeeper so he has all the information needed to ship the bottles.

"Sir," he says, "Perhaps you would like to buy a few more bottles of oil. It won't cost you any more because the minimum freight charge is 40 Euros for a kilo."

*"Well,"* I think, *"It will cost me more for the oil, but not to ship them, so let's go for it. We can always surprise others with a bottle of olive oil from Lucca that they'll never find in their specialty store."*

Sandra and I get four more bottles which, when all are packaged together, total just under one kilogram. He carefully fills out the shipping documents and gives me a receipt.

"You should get them in three to four weeks. Thank you very much," he says, bows slightly, and puts the box on a table behind him.

We step into the street and continue to the bus rendezvous, happy to have more Christmas gifts ticked off our list and not have to pack them in our luggage for the trip home. The less we have to take through customs the better.

Just outside the gate where we had entered Lucca is a small park where the others will join us to walk to the bus. With the only bench taken by some locals, we find seats on the ruins of a foundation poking through the grass. Based on the terra cotta rubble in the middle and the marble on the exterior of the wall fragments, I guess this was part of a Roman building, long abandoned and now mostly fallen or torn down. It is a pleasant wait in the shade, with a very light breeze that flits by just often enough to cool the sweat accumulating on my back. Locals bustle purposefully through the gates. Tourists stumble out with packages in their arms, bewildered as they get their bearings and decide where to go next.

Our small group finally assembles, and the tour guide leads us to the waiting bus and the drive back to the ship. The large cruise ship has departed, so the Viking *Sky* looks bigger than it did before.

We eat in the World Café as the ship leaves Livorno and then go to the Star Theater for a lecture about our next stop: Monaco. Every day in late afternoon they brief us on the next day's stop and tours. We hear a brief history of the city-state. One person asks about Grace Kelly who was in several movies, the last of which was "The Swan" about a young princess who is encouraged to marry the handsome crown prince. This is exactly what Grace Kelly did in real life, gaining 142 official titles which were recited at her civil wedding ceremony. A very British man pipes up and takes nearly five minutes to point out, in a rather disparaging and condescending tone, that "Princess Grace, the beautiful actress and wife of Prince Rainier who rules Monaco, was not a royal and could never be addressed as 'Your Royal Highness' but only as 'Your Serene Highness' because Monaco is a Principality, not a monarchy. A principality does not have royalty. Only monarchies have royalty that includes Kings and Queens. In principalities the highest you can go is Prince and Princess." I guess to some people, or at least one person, the distinction is important. What I really want to know is what were the 142 official titles for Princess Grace? Just reciting them must have taken a significant portion of the civil ceremony.

# 4 – COASTING ALONG

## MONACO

Spoiler alert: Monaco is not an inexpensive place to visit. Fees to tie up to a dock start at €1,200 per half-day — for each meter of the boat. There are additional charges for power, water, sewage, etc. The *Viking Sky* moors at one of the buoys in the harbor, which is much less expensive, and we take the ship's skiff (actually one of the lifeboats) to and from the shore. This appears on the itinerary as "tendering." The Mediterranean is a bit choppy this morning with one- to two-foot waves which reflect off the ship, so we have to carefully time stepping from the ship onto the bobbing boat, trying to make the transition just at the peak of a bob when the boat pauses for a split second before descending and moving away from the ship. It makes for an interesting start and end to the excursions.

Sandra and I forego walking around the shops or going into the casino to see how quickly we can lose money in either. Instead, we opt to take a special tour of the Villa Rothschild at the edge of the city-state. Paul, the driver, expertly threads the bus through the winding streets lined with Lamborghinis, Ferraris, Rolls Royces, Bentleys, Porches, Mercedes, and other expensive cars which occasionally pull out directly in front of the bus as if it could stop on a dime. Farther from the port itself, the road is scratched from the side of the mountains with bicycles, motorbikes, scooters, and cars alike careening along as if they are the only vehicles around. After a few minutes of watching the mayhem that Paul calmly negotiates, we look out the windows at the wonderful views of the blue Mediterranean with a few puffy white clouds floating serenely above and sailboats dotting the horizon. With the mountains plunging directly into the sea, most houses are perched on ledges, either natural or man-made, with personal views of the water and almost no views of their neighbors except for rooftops below.

## VILLA ET JARDINS EPHRUSSI DE ROTHSCHILD

We arrive at Cap Ferrat, get off the bus, and climb a rather steep driveway to the gate of the Villa et Jardins Ephrussi de Rothschild[6] with a sign that admonishes guests to leave the premises before it closes automatically at 6:30 pm. There's no indication what will happen if you miss the closing, but it does not seem likely they will invite you inside for the night.

The main building front is two stories tall. Originally entirely ochre yellow with white trim, it is now inexplicably Barbi-doll pink with white trim while only a bay window

---

[6] See https://www.villa-ephrussi.com/en

surrounding a staircase at the left end retains the original color scheme. The windows with wooden shutters closed against the heat are recessed in the thick walls, allowing space for "French balconies" at each. This provides room for the shutters to be opened outward and folded to let in light and breezes, but there is no room to stand on the balcony. The first-floor windows and doorways have pointed Gothic arches and elaborate tracery above, while the second-floor windows have smooth Roman arches, and the attic windows are simple small squares. Here at the entryway, we meet our Villa guide, Jacqueline, who speaks very clear English, probably because she's from Essex, England, and attended Cambridge.

The rooms in the house are each decorated in different styles and highlight different art forms. One, for example, with ornate white plaster walls features an extensive porcelain collection while another with red walls features paintings by old masters. Each room is wildly different, with no real unifying theme among the rooms, but each is internally consistent. All the floors are parquet inlaid in elaborate patterns which differ from room to room.

We are rather hustled through the house itself to the expansive gardens in the back. The gravel semicircle and wide path leading from the house to the gardens are currently set up for a wedding dinner, or at least a wedding dinner photoshoot. A bride's table with two chairs and place settings faces a long guest table with twenty-four chairs and place settings. All have white linens, napkins, and chairs. The three photographers and model bride are a bit irritated that we are interrupting their shoot, so we move quickly past them and into the gardens proper.

Béatrice Rothschild, daughter of the baron Alphonse de Rothschild and Leonora Rothschild (of the English branch of the extended family), married Maurice Ephrussi in 1883, but they divorced in 1904 after she contracted an illness from Maurice which prevented her bearing children, and his gambling debts had grown to over 12 million gold francs. When her father died in 1905, Béatrice inherited his immense fortune and decided to build her dream villa in Cap Ferrat. When she discovered that King Léopold II of Belgium was also interested in the land, she immediately purchased it without any further negotiation and started construction. The site, which sits atop a hill on a peninsula overlooking the Mediterranean Sea, was largely rocky — not very suitable for the gardens she envisioned — so she had the ground dynamited and huge volumes of dirt brought in. Completed in 1912, the villa and gardens were her winter home until shortly before her death in 1934.

Legend has it that soon after Béatrice bought the site she invited herself to dinner at a neighbor's place that was below hers. After some appetizers and pleasantries, she asked the neighbor, "How much do you want for this villa?"

"Well, I haven't thought about selling it."

"I very much want to buy it."

"But you have the much larger villa on the top of the hill. Why do you want this place as well?"

"Oh. Your house blocks part of the view of the sea and harbor from my garden."

"How would buying my house solve your vista problem?"

"I would tear it down, of course, so my view would be unimpeded."

"Well, in that case, it's not for sale."

It is said they never visited each other again and avoided each other socially whenever possible.

We stroll through the gardens, each with different collections of plants: French, Spanish, Florentine, stone, Japanese, exotic, Provençal, and rose. Several include ponds or streams connecting with ponds from other areas. Béatrice was very particular about exactly where each plant and water feature should be. There are stories of employees laying out long strips of carpet so she could precisely position the paths and streams, and of servants hiding inside tall green cardboard cones to place each of the trees. Benches encourage us to sit in the shade and contemplate peaceful views of the Mediterranean and hills. From one bench we see a red tile roof and whitewashed wall blocking our view of the shoreline immediately below, but we do see several sailboats serenely plying the placid waters off the peninsula.

The transition from one garden to the next is somehow both subtle and obvious. As we walk along the path the vegetation changes in both scale and color until we suddenly realize we are in a different type of garden. It's quite a wonderful experience, especially with the gentle breeze from the sea bringing a suggestion of salt air to the fragrances of the flowers and keeping the hot sun at bay.

After several hours exploring the gardens, we walk down the steep hill to the waiting bus and Paul adroitly maneuvers it through the narrow winding streets back to the dock where we will board the tender for the short trip to the ship. As we arrive, we see one of our tenders leaving, so we wait for the next one, which should be only fifteen minutes or so.

## SS SYMPHONY

There are many magnificent yachts tied up to the piers, and some of them are anchored in the inner harbor. Since it is very crowded, boats do not use their own anchors but instead tie up to anchor points already placed in the harbor floor. Divers connect the lines from the ships to the anchor points. When there are divers in the water, tenders and other surface craft are not allowed to be in the area. When our tender is clear of the inner harbor, a large yacht, the *SS Symphony* from Georgetown, pulls up to one of the nearby anchorages, turns around, and backs into an anchorage spot. Now a boat comes out with two divers, and they take lines from the yacht down to the anchor spots. There are no buoys, so the divers must locate the tie-downs in the murky water. This takes about forty-five minutes, during which time no other boats are allowed in the area. Now secured, the yacht owner decides he wants to be closer so he can extend a gangway from the stern of his boat to the pier instead of having to use a dinghy to get ashore. The divers return, release the anchor lines, the yacht backs ten feet closer to the pier, and the divers connect the lines to new tie-downs underwater. We wait another forty-five minutes while the *SS Symphony* finally settles in place and the divers get out of the water so our tender boat can come in and pick us up.

While I am irritated by the delay in my travels caused by a billionaire insisting on just the perfect mooring spot, the *SS Symphony* is a beautiful ship. Sleek and smooth, even while anchored it seems anxious to get underway. It's like watching a sheep dog that just wants to go herd sheep instead of sitting by its master. Owned by Bernard Arnault,

CEO of Moët Hennessy–Louis Vuitton, the sleek 333-foot-long ship is a floating palace for 20 passengers and a crew of 38 (a 1.9 crew to passenger ratio, over double that of our very comfortable Viking *Sky*). Unlike many other super-yachts which spend most of their time in one port, this one travels extensively around the world. I'm a bit awed by its beauty and, as a sailor at heart, happy that the *Symphony* frequently sails on the high seas. It would be a shame to see the ship's spirit tied to a dock for long.

Our tender is finally able to pick us up and we cross the rather choppy water to the ship. Getting off the tender is more of a challenge than earlier. The waves are a bit higher and coming from many angles off the scalloped shoreline as well as from the open sea, making the small tender boat bob up and down very irregularly one to two feet as we approach the ship. We time our jump from tender to ship during the half second that the tender pauses at the peak of a wave, with the crew grabbing our arms and pulling us into the ship.

# 5 – MARSEILLE

Marseille[7] is the third largest city in France with many hills and a large port naturally protected from storm waves by a curving peninsula. The area was inhabited for over 30,000 years by small groups and established as a city by Greeks around 600 BCE as Massalia. Since then, it has had its ups and downs, but largely retained its place as a major transshipment point for goods from across the Mediterranean. Exports were primarily French oils and wine to places as far away as Ur in southeastern Mesopotamia and Thebes in Egypt, as well as most Mediterranean coastal cities such as Rome, Carthage, Syracuse, Alexandria, Athens, and nearby cities on the Iberian Peninsula. Imports included leather and skins, ceramics, fish, spices, papyrus, cookware, grains, and other commodities and luxury items. These were either shipped North into the rest of Gaul (later called France) or traded within their extensive network around the Mediterranean Sea. Some may recall that Marseille was portrayed as a hub of drug trafficking in the movie *The*

---

[7] See https://www.marseille.fr/ for extensive information and detailed history. There is no English version of the website (unlike most European websites) so you'll have to rely the Google translation unless you read French.

*French Connection,* but drugs are a tiny tiny portion of the current trade.

"La Marseillaise," the song that 500 local volunteers sang calling the populace to fight tyranny in 1792 while marching to Paris during the French Revolution, has been in and out of favor many times. A rallying song for the Revolution was subsequently banned by Napoleon and King Louis XVIII before being reinstated in 1830. Napoleon III banned it again before it was again reinstated in 1879 when it was finally declared the official French national anthem in their constitution.

The group takes a walking tour around the city center. The hills look pleasant and inviting but are surprisingly steep once we try to keep up with Maria, the tour leader. Those of us who are older and slower find we are constantly walking, while the younger, fitter people surge ahead with her and get to rest while waiting for us to catch up. Just before we do catch up, Maria takes off again. I feel a donkey being enticed by a carrot to keep moving. Our earpieces keep us informed of her insights, bits of history, and directions if we stay within two hundred or so feet of her. She leads us through shaded residential streets lined with both narrow townhouses and villas with gardens and gated entries. All the houses have French balconies at the windows above the ground floor, enabling them to let in the cool evening breezes and keep out the hot midday and afternoon sun. Well, we are in France, so of course they have French balconies. At the moment, the shutters are all closed.

We pass several plazas and street intersections with triumphal arches. These were mostly built by people who defeated Marseille rather than celebrating wins by Marseille. I find they all look pretty much alike: massive square pillars connected by a tall wide massive arch with sculptures of horses, men, and battle equipment. The celebratory inscriptions are written in Latin with Vs instead of Us, and the letter J did not yet exist making them even harder to read. Who is Ivlivs Caesar? And the dates take several minutes to figure out because it's in some convoluted combination of Roman letters instead of number. Really, what year is MCDXLVIII?

Back in the city center, we have some free time to explore on our own.[8] At first it seems like a sleepy city, but do not be fooled; there is a lot to see, do, and eat. Sandra and I decide to visit a museum, of which there are over a dozen, including a Children's Museum. We usually seek out the children's museum because their displays are often interactive, making the visit more interesting, and the explanations are aimed right at our level of understanding.

---

[8] See THE 15 BEST Things to Do in Marseille (2024) - Must-See Attractions (tripadvisor.com) for other places to see, things to do, and places to dine and sleep in Marseille.

# MUSÉE DES DOCKS ROMAINS

We end up going to the Musée des Docks Romains at 10 Place de Vivaux because it's close and looks small enough to tour in the hour or so until we must return to the boat. Digging to build a parking structure in the 1950s revealed artifacts of the port dating from Roman times. These finds resulted in abandoning the plans for a parking structure and archaeological excavations began, ultimately resulting in the Musée des Docks Romains. There is now a park of about an acre with the remains of ancient docks and anchors. At one side of the park is a commercial building and the maritime museum[9]. Inside the museum there are extensive displays of the amphorae and other types of jars and containers for oils, wine, and spices.

The ribs and hull planks that were embedded in the mud are all that remains of two boats found by the pier. Each boat is twenty to thirty feet long and eight to ten feet wide with a broad and shallow draft suitable for shuttling goods between ships and shore. There is no evidence of a mast, so these were probably rowed.

Amphorae seem silly. They were used for many centuries and have mystified me for nearly as long. They

---

[9] The Musée des Docks romains at 10, Place Vivaux, 13002 Marseille, France https://musees.marseille.fr/muse-des-docks-romains-0

seem to have been the bulk containers of their day. The jars have two long handles, one on either side of a thin neck connecting the almond-shaped bottom to the opening at the top. They are often very large, holding five to perhaps fifty gallons of liquid; I've never seen a one-quart amphora. The very bottom is usually tapered to a blunt point so that if it's standing up it must be carefully balanced or held by some support to keep from falling over. This seems very impractical to me; a container that you can't set down. Outdoors they might be jammed into the ground or a hole, but what do you do inside? Lean the amphora in a corner hoping it won't slide down the wall? Create a special hook for hanging the amphora? Or just have a servant/slave stand there holding it upright? There are some amphorae in three-legged stands with a horizontal ring in which the vessel is suspended by its base. Some scholars justify their shape by noting they can be stowed tightly against each other for shipping, but that's true only if they all are the same size, and most of the amphorae on display are of different sizes. Even amphorae of the same size do not stack snugly with one another. They are bound together in custom racks to keep them from moving around during shipping.[10] And they all tip over on their own, so if they're not tightly plugged most of the contents spill out.

**Figure 5 Amphorae**

A large model of Marseille as it might have appeared in the Middle Ages draws our attention. There are tall and

---

[10] Please see https://archaeologydataservice.ac.uk/archives/view/amphora_ahrb_2005/index.cfm for additional archaeological information about the history, variations, and classifications of amphorae.

extensive stone walls protecting the city on all sides except the ocean with the docks and beaches (which also were used for loading and unloading boats). There is a surprisingly large collection of glassware, both clear and tinted, in a variety of shapes: mostly with bulbous bottoms and narrow necks. Drinking glasses and cups, vials, which I suppose held perfumes or ointments, and bowls rounded out the collection. The ceramic objects reflect styles and decorations from the breadth of the Mediterranean. Also included in the display are many ossuaries (bone boxes) and grave markers from a cemetery at the edge of the harbor. These all honor and remember the dead, and we pause to consider that we, too, will end up being indistinguishable from them.

On our way back to the ship, we pass by the Château d'If[11] which is the primary setting for Alexandre Dumas's *The Count of Monte Cristo*. The chateau, which is a castle fortress, covers nearly the entire Île d'Ilf, the smallest island in the Frioul archipelago just outside the harbor. Sitting nearly a mile offshore and surrounded by swift swirling currents, which shift quickly as the tide comes in and goes out, the castle served well as a prison from which there is no documented successful escape, notwithstanding the imagination of Monsieur Dumas.

---

[11] See https://www.chateau-if.fr

# 6 - MONTPELLIER

Unlike many American cities and towns which take their name from a city in Great Britain or Ireland, Montpelier, the capital of Vermont, was named after Montpellier, France, because of the French support for the American colonies during the Revolutionary War. Today we visit the French namesake which nestles against the mountains at the south edge of the country. An import center for spices in the 10th century, it gained the University of Montpellier in 1220 which soon began to emphasize secular studies including law and medicine. Now the city is headquarters for the International Vine and Wine Fair and is the administrative center for the Languedoc region, famous for its wines. The French are notorious for demanding their individual freedom and protesting any regulation or restriction by the central government, even if it is good for them.

*"Only peril can bring the French together. One can't impose unity out of the blue on a country that has 265 kinds of cheese."*

*- Charles de Gaulle*

# CHÂTEAU FLAUGERGUES

We have never been to a château before and look forward to experiencing a classic French country house. We join a group for a tour of the Château Flaugergues[12] just outside Montpellier. Unlike many of the other sites we visit in southern France, the château itself has no Roman heritage although some of its grapevines may date to Roman times. Construction began in 1696 by Etienne de Flaugergues and continued for over forty-five years. Also called a "Folly," the chateau was a "pleasure house," originally occupied for only three months each year. The Colbert family (I do not know if they are related to the comic Steven Colbert), Flaugergues' descendants, have lived here year-round for the last 320 years. Its website calls it "the castle and its gardens," which is a bit of an exaggeration to my mind. Mansion, yes. Stately home, yes. Manor, yes. Country house, yes. Possibly even a palace if royalty had ever lived there; but it has none of the characteristics generally associated with a castle. There is no moat, no defensive wall, no towers, no fortifications of any type. "A man's home is his castle" does not make every home a castle. It is an attractive country house and worth the time to see it and its gardens and vineyards and to sample its wines.

---

[12] Website https://www.flaugergues.com

We approach the château through its formal French garden which extends a hundred fifty feet or so from the house. Tall thin cedar trees line the sides of the garden, with the entry terrace and house forming the far end. A packed gravel path and shoulder-high box hedges define each side of the garden with its closely cut grass and symmetrically placed sculptures, several fountains, and two semi-circular paths which meet in the center. Wide staircases from each side of the French garden lead to a large terrace in front of the main entrance to the three-story house with a brown tile roof. All the windows have blue wood shutters now closed to the midday sun and heat. A modest solid double door entry leads to a broad open marble staircase that winds up to all three floors, leaving an expansive atrium that is nearly one quarter of the whole house. The six-foot wide staircase extends directly from the walls with no columns, instead using hanging key vaults for support. During construction one of the steps leading to the third floor cracked and shifted nearly an inch and a half, but it has not moved since then, so it seems to be safe. The house is only one room deep, so the staircase leads directly to rooms on either side of the atrium, rather than to halls. Since the Colbert family still lives here, we bypass most of the rooms.

19th century tapestries from the Flemish workshop of Philippe Wauters line several walls depicting classical,

Christian, and Napoleonic scenes. Many are faded from exposure to sunlight over the years, but the original brilliance is seen in some folds. The blues and reds are particularly vibrant.

The walls of the master bedroom are painted with fanciful scenes of Napoleon's invasion of Egypt (1798-1801). So detailed are the images that one could almost imagine the wall panels as windows looking out at Cairo, the pyramids, and the sands of Egypt — complete with a fly and a bee (one of Napoleon's icons) carefully rendered on the window/walls. Paintings of open curtains adorn the sides of each panel. Little soldiers with flags peek out from behind the painted curtains. Opposite the bed is a vanity that also encloses a doll house, complete with a miniature of the carpet that is on the floor directly in front of the vanity.

Leaving the back of the house via larger French doors, we encounter the much larger and more varied private gardens. A bit of ivy clings to the house walls. Palmetto and tall date palms grace the path toward the 400-meter-long alley of olive trees. Scattered throughout are trees from around the world: ginkgo biloba, cork oak, sequoia, and others. On the hill we see the vineyards, source of the wine we will soon sample. At the end of the walk, we enter a bamboo forest which shades us from the intense sun and provides a calm cool sanctuary for the wine tasting.

## WINE TASTING

This is an interesting ritual, especially among enophiles. The idea is that we have a small sip of each wine to help us decide which ones we like and find so rapturous we cannot help but purchase several bottles — or cases. The ritual begins with the vintner describing the provenance of the vines. This is the history of where the vines originated and traveled before arriving here. It's like tracing your ancestry to the first voyage of the Mayflower or to Genghis Khan. The story might be something like: "Our vines were first discovered clinging to the rocky coast of southern Crete by early Phoenician sailors in the second millennium BCE. They took cuttings and started small vineyards in the Levant. Centuries later Julias Caesar and his armies carried some root stock to Montpellier where it flourished in the rocky soil. That is why the Languedoc-Roussillon region, where we are, is now the largest wine producing area in the world, making more than Australia or Chile or South Africa.[13]"

---

[13] Refer to Languedoc Wine: Map, Regions, Grape Varieties, History and more - Social Vignerons

The vintner (they dislike the plebian term *'winemaker,'* but will beam proudly if you call them an *'oenologist'* or even more impressively *'vigneron.'*) goes on to describe how they grow the grapes and how they must suffer to produce great wine. Suffering is caused by rocky soil, minimal rain, hot sun, wind, and on and on. The vigneron evidently suffers right along with the grapes. While describing the grapes, they (for there are many female as well as male vignerons) usually refer to types of grapes we know about, like Syrah, Grenache, or Cabernet, but rarely mention the other types essential to their particular blend, such as Viognier, Carignan, or Mourvèdre.

After the elaborate description of the provenance of the grapes and the difficulties of making any wine at all, we move on to the audience participation portion of the ritual. Three or four types of wine are elaborately displayed along with recitation of the awards that each has won. If a wine is presented that has not won some award it is likely the reputed source of a miraculous healing. Usually there is at least one red, a white, and a rosé, each with a different amount of residual sugar. From the least sweet to the sweetest we have six levels: *'bone dry,'* *'dry,'* *'off-dry,'* *'semi-sweet,'* *'sweet,'* and *'very sweet.'* This seems straightforward, although I'm not certain why less sweet is called "drier." Perhaps it is because the least sweet wines, those with almost no residual sugar, leave my mouth feeling dehydrated. Different languages have different words for each level of sweetness, often including additional qualifications and with different residual sugar levels. German wines, for instance are generally in four levels: 'Trocken,' 'Halbtrocken' (or 'Feinherb'), 'Liebliche,' and 'Süss.' Then, just to complicate matters even more, sparkling wines and champagne are described in eight levels: 'brut nature,' 'extra brut,' 'brut,' 'extra dry,' 'dry' (or 'sec'), 'demi-sec,' and 'doux.'[14] Many of the oenophile's terms seem designed to intimidate the uninitiated so they will simply accept a sommelier's assertion that this is a great wine. Even if it is best suited to accompany oil as a salad dressing.

Now that the wine is here, they bring out the glasses. These are long-stemmed tulip glasses which we hold by the base or the stem to prevent the heat from our hands warming the wine and changing its flavor profile. Along with the stemware are large tumblers of water and a large empty jar which we'll get to in a moment.

Several assistants pour a large splash of the first wine, which is the dryest we will sample, into our tulip glass, probably an ounce or two. We start with the dryest so we will be able to taste the increasing levels of

[14] Refer to https://winefolly.com and The Ultimate Wine Sweetness Chart: The Sweet Scale (sloshspot.com)

sweetness. If we start with the sweetest, some residual sugar in our mouth would carry over from one glass to the next. We now follow the vigneron's directions.

"Carefully swirl the wine in the glass. Do not shake it. Swirl the wine around the inside and watch how it slides down the glass when you stop swirling. This shows you the great legs[15] of our wine.

"Now hold the glass up to the light and observe the color and clarity of the wine. It should be fully transparent with no cloudiness."

Next, we swirl the wine again, put our nose into the glass, and inhale sharply. This gives us the wine's bouquet. It also prepares our olfactory senses for what is to come, sort of like an appetizer.

Having taken in the bouquet, we can now sip a small amount of wine but must keep it in our mouth. No swallowing during a wine tasting.

"Keeping the wine in your mouth, suck in air over the wine, aerating it to release its flavors.

"Slosh it around. Mix it with your saliva and sense the changes in aromas and taste. Close your eyes to help concentrate the intensity and complexity of the flavors."

---

[15] See Glossary of Wine Tasting Terms And Their Meaning (sommelierschoiceawards.com) for wine vocabulary.

Now we spit the wine into the large empty jar, although a few of us swallow the wine now that we have spent so much time and effort evaluating it.

"Now take a moment to evaluate the taste that remains in your mouth. This is the finish."

"Now rinse your mouth with the water to prepare it for the next wine."

We repeat the whole ritual for each wine: pouring, swirling, ogling legs, checking color and clarity, sniffing the bouquet, slurping the wine, aerating and sloshing it, spitting it out, and evaluating its "finish."

Some people comment at great length about the flavors and aromas they believe they experienced.

"Undertones of peach and hints of jasmine and hibiscus with a nutty earthy finish."

"Slightly acidic and a bit aggressive for my likes, but certainly full bodied with backbone and a bit raisiny."

"Very round, a bit reticent, but supple, toasty, and tight."

"Wonderful nose and very opulent and round."

Right.

I like the second wine, which is a semi-sweet rosé. Not particularly dazzling (my socks remained on my feet) but it would serve well as a drink to accompany almost any meal. This is, after all, the primary reason to make wine.

While the wine tasting ritual is interesting, I find it is also a bit pretentious. Watching people at meals and just relaxing together, I very rarely see anyone swirling, ogling legs, checking color and clarity, sniffing the bouquet, slurping the wine, aerating and sloshing their wine; they just wash food down with it or sip it during a conversation.

Just slightly tipsy from the wine coupled with the heat, we return to the ship and have a needed afternoon nap.

# 7 - BARCELONA

## ARRIVAL

We dock in Barcelona and soon find ourselves riding down its tree-lined divided boulevards with a variety of apartments, houses, and stores with living quarters above. All have French balconies and wooden shutters on the windows above the ground floor. Usually stone at street level, the upper floors are either brick or stucco with the occasional all-stone mansion. Medians with fifty-foot-tall trees, shoulder-high bushes, and very modern sleek LED streetlights separate the broad sidewalks from the streets. Decorative concrete plinths support ornate bronze objects that look like they might have once been cauldrons of burning oil to illuminate the mid-block crosswalks. Each of the cauldrons is different, supported by griffins, dragons, and other fantastical creatures as well as Titans, snakes, and plants.

## LA SAGRADA FAMILIA – PART 1

We get off the bus, walk through a park, and circle the new cathedral which has been under construction since March 19, 1882. Formally "El Templo Expiatorio de la Sagrada Familia," it's commonly called simply "Sagrada

Familia" or "Sacred Family Church."[16] It may be the only UNESCO Heritage Site that is still under construction.

The original design by Francisco de Paula del Villar was a traditional neo-Gothic building with ogival windows, buttresses, a pointed bell tower, and a dome with tower over the intersection of the nave and transept. Budget and technical issues soon led to Antoni Gaudi taking over in 1883. Gaudi developed a radically different plan using shapes from nature, soaring spiral spires, and no flat walls. He guided construction until his death in 1926. A succession of seven other architects led the project over the next ninety-six years, all following Gaudi's plans. This is very unique; most cathedrals that take many decades to build undergo design changes in the interim; sometimes minor, sometimes major, and often influenced by finances and political events. The Chapel of Saint Joseph is the first discrete portion of the building completed and the first masses were held in 1885. During the Spanish Civil War in 1936, the building was vandalized and the plaster models Gaudi developed to help engineer the novel shapes and necessary supports were smashed. Construction resumed after the Civil War using published plans and photographs of the models, and the engineering design workshop was rebuilt. This was one of the first buildings for which

---

[16] See https://sagradafamilia.org/en for tickets and additional information.

models were built for every element to test their structural integrity and develop the appropriate construction techniques.

When we are there in July, 2022, it is still incomplete but very impressive. "Impressive" alone does not adequately describe its emotional, visual, and intellectual impact. Awe-inspiring? Humbling? Stunning? Breath-taking? Majestic? Odd? All are appropriate.

There are eight spiral-like towers at either end of the transept. Above the nave, which is the tallest in Europe, are the four towers of the Evangelists, each 135 meters tall, with the tower of the Virgin Mary at 134 meters over the intersection of the nave and transept. The tallest, the tower of Jesus Christ, will soar to 138 meters above the altar when completed in 2026. The tallest point on the basilica will be two meters lower in elevation than the peak of the tallest mountain surrounding Barcelona because Gaudi reportedly said, "Man should not try building higher than God."

Today we walk around the exterior which is surrounded by masses of people on all sides. The sidewalks on both sides of the street are completely filled with people, forcing us at times to step into the street and risk injury from the many mopeds, motorcycles, and cars. We will need to get tickets to go inside, but for now are content to gaze in awe at this tall, organic structure unlike any other cathedral we have seen. The grey-tan stone and concrete make the building look like it is being ejected out of the earth rather than being built on it. Like Gothic cathedrals, symbolism is everywhere; but here it's on steroids. Every nook and cranny on the outside has a Biblical reference. The style might be called "Modern Baroque" for the extensive ornamentation of every surface.

To the left of the "passion entrance" is a modern sculpture of Judas betraying Jesus with a kiss. Next to this is a "magic square" in which each row, column, and major diagonal have numbers that add to thirty-three, Jesus' age when he died. Slightly to its right is a partly displaced column with a man roped to it who could either be Jesus being scourged or, since the column is displaced, it could be Samson pulling down the pillar of the Philistine temple.

**Figure 6 Detail of exterior, La Sagrada Familia**

Above the door are two sculptures. The lower one is a scene with Jesus carrying his cross on the right side and what could be the Roman centurions on the left side, although they are dressed more like Star Wars storm troopers. In front of this scene is Mary looking down with an image of Jesus on the cape she's holding. Above this tableau is the scene of Jesus on the cross with a skull at the base and four women weeping at His feet. All these characters' faces are rendered in surrealist fashion with no attempt to portray actual people, which I find adds to the intensity of the scene because I'm not distracted by facial details but engrossed by their emotions.

Above the "nativity entrance" on the opposite side of the cathedral are scenes of Jesus' birth. In the center Mary washes the baby in a tub while Joseph and some vague animals look on. Above them are people smiling and looking down at Jesus, Mary, and Joseph. Above them are two angels playing instruments that were certainly not part of the nativity: a pedal harp and a bassoon. Even higher up is Jesus casting the demon out of the prostitute flanked on the right and left by four angels blowing herald trumpets. The highest scene is of Jesus crowning someone (possibly Peter) as another man kneels in adoration. Oddly, the arch surrounding this highest tableau looks like the jaws and teeth of a great white shark. At the very top of this spire, doves fly from the cathedral into the world.

To the right of Mary, Jesus, and Joseph, are four shepherds looking on, one with a lamb draped over his neck, while other sheep graze below them. To the left are the three magi kneeling and presenting their gifts. Above the magi are two people playing a lute and a violin (again, instruments not present in 1 CE). Even farther to the left is a Roman soldier about to impale a baby as its mother on her knees pleads to the Centurian as another dead baby lies on the ground draped over the edge. Below the woman are three geese whose meaning I'm not certain of. Surrounding all these scenes are twisted vines and branches evoking the tree of life.

The spires which soar above the main building are round with what appear to be small balconies of apartments — perhaps alluding to a mansion with many rooms. "Sanctus" is inscribed multiple times around each spire.

The more I look at the details, the more Biblical references I see. Some are very subtle allusions: vaguely dove-like pimples on a wall; while others are more obvious, such as projections that evoke praying or pleading hands reaching skyward. There are vertical rows of skulls; or are they seashells? Hiding in the open are statues and busts. The sculptors, like those who carved gargoyles on Gothic cathedrals, seem to have been given free rein to create images and allusions to Biblical stories and people, but everything is integrated into a coherent, if sometimes hard to decipher, whole. Nothing seems out of place, even if it also seems a bit odd at first sight.

I could spend days examining the exterior, constantly finding new details and pondering the meaning of each and of the whole. We must get tickets to go inside, but the rest of today is sold out, so we return to the ship and prepare to transition to the Nobu Hotel for our two-day extension in Barcelona before returning home.

At noon we leave the ship and check into the hotel and go to the concierge to get tickets for the Sagrada Familia. This takes a lot longer than expected. The church's and the hotel's internet trade connectivity issues and slow response times, sometimes resulting in losing all data entered. We start again. One time we have a reservation mostly complete, but when we increase the number of tickets to two the site says none are available for that time. Reservations for a week or more in the future are easy to get, but by then we'll be back home in California. Reservations for two for today are impossible; we settle for the earliest we can get: tomorrow at 2:00 pm. The lesson: book admission several weeks in advance. Our two tickets are €54.60. Not cheap, but most of the price goes toward the cathedral's construction costs. It's nearly 5 pm when we finish getting the tickets, so we head to the hotel's restaurant for dinner and then upstairs (well, up elevator) for a good night's sleep.

# DAY 2

## MUSEU NACIONAL D'ARTE DE CATALUNYA

Since we won't be able to go into the Sagrada Familia until 2 pm, we take a taxi to the Museu Nacional d'Arte de Catalunya[17] which sits atop one of the hills overlooking Barcelona. This is an expansive and imposing building which initially strikes me as a seat of government. A huge central section with a tall dome is flanked on either side by long multi-story wings. The driver drops us off at the bottom of a very long and wide staircase leading to the museum. From the bottom, it looks like perhaps 100 steps; halfway up it seems like there are now 500. Slightly out of breath from the climb, we go inside and find the ticket booth — at the top of even more steps. Good news! Since we're over sixty-five and there's a lot of steps in the museum, we get in for free. It turns out that this museum is wonderful, well worth more than the three hours we have available.

One section of the museum particularly attracts our attention because it displays frescos rescued from walls of deteriorating churches throughout Catalonia. There is no practical way to preserve the frescos *in situ*, so the museum developed a technique to apply paper

---

[17] See https://www.museunacional.cat/en

impregnated with a solution that loosens the thin layer of plaster in which the fresco is painted and remove the paint and plaster together and intact. They place the salvaged fresco in a full-scale mock-up of the wall on which the fresco had been. This preserves the paint and plaster which would crack if it were laid flat. They install the wall mock-up with the salvaged fresco in the museum where it is now in a temperature and humidity-controlled environment which keeps the fragile fresco from further failure. They did not attempt restoring the frescos by imagining what was in the places where the paint had already fallen off. Restoring a fresco is very difficult in part because it's hard to match the pigments (modern ones may have the same initial color but if not made of the same materials, change over time). The curators opted to simply conserve them in the condition they were found, although they did remove centuries of accumulated soot and grime revealing oftentimes brilliant colors and delicate brushwork.

Frescos have been used for over two millennia to decorate walls. It's a well-tested technique, but it does have its long-term challenges and limitations. It is very labor intensive to make. First the artist draws sketches of the scene on paper, working out the details in pencil, chalk, or ink. When satisfied the drawing is correct, they or an apprentice make a cartoon of it: a scaled enlargement that is the size the scene will appear on the wall or ceiling. Now the artist must make the pigments to be used; find the minerals and plants and grind them into an extremely fine powder. Pre-made pigments were not available until the late nineteenth century. Now they are ready to begin work on the wall. First, they apply a thin layer of wet plaster to the wall or ceiling. All remaining steps must be completed before the plaster dries, so only an area that can be painted in less than a day is prepared. Then the cartoon of the art is placed against the wall and is punctured along the images' edges before dust or a similar fine-grained material is blown or patted against it, leaving a faint line on the plaster when the cartoon is removed. While the outline is being made on the wall, the artist finishes making the paint by mixing the finely ground pigments with the proper amount of egg yolk to make tempera. Then begins a sort of paint-by-numbers process filling in the appropriate colors within the lines from the cartoon's impression. They had to work rather quickly because the tempera paint dries quickly.[18] This, coupled with its opacity, limits their ability to do subtle shading and blending of colors, but the paint is absorbed into the wet plaster, making the image a part of the wall itself, not just a coating on the surface. They made more paint as needed

---

[18] While Leonardo did experiment with oil-based paint on some frescos, it did not turn out well and he abandoned the technique.

during the day since the tempera dries more quickly than the plaster.

When the plaster and paint have dried, they begin the process again: apply wet plaster where the next part of the scene will be, outline the image using the cartoon, mix the paint, fill in the outlines, mix more paint as needed, and wait for the plaster to dry. This process, while providing often brilliant and saturated colors, also introduces mechanical instability in the artwork which leads to its partial disintegration over time without frequent maintenance. The thin plaster with the paint may not be uniform and thus dry at different rates, causing paint absorption and adhesion issues. Moisture in the air and/or the surface under the fresco may cause it to separate from the underlying wall. Mold growing in the painted plaster layer can physically break the plaster with its tiny tendrils, much like a tree breaking a sidewalk. Once a fresco starts deteriorating, it often goes downhill rapidly.

The first fresco we encounter in the museum, although incomplete, clearly depicts the stoning of St. Stephen, the first martyr. Depictions of the stoning are very sanitized and almost never show its gruesomeness. Steven is typically shown kneeling as he prays and several men stand about with brick-sized stones raised over their heads or, as in this fresco, the stones are flying through the air but have not hit Stephen. Stoning, in my mind, is a particularly hypocritical method of execution because it allows the killer executioners to distance themselves from the act and each can claim it was not their stone that killed the victim.

**Figure 7 Recovered fresco of stoning of St. Stephen**

The Talmud specifies that the victim first be thrown off a height; if that does not kill him (or her) then a large stone is dropped on their chest; and only if they survive that do bystanders throw stones until the person is dead. Some other stoning laws specify that the condemned first be buried up to their waist (or chest for women) in a ditch before stoning using stones "small enough that the person cannot be killed by only one or two stones."

Other frescos illustrate various New Testament stories: the annunciation of Mary, Madonna with child, nativity, and the crucifixion (another very slow and painful torture death). There is a scene of Moses holding the Ten Commandment stones aloft, ready to smash them as he sees the people worshiping a golden calf. Most of the frescos are on curved walls and niches, some with window openings that are also frescoed. Standing close to the meticulously recreated walls, curves, and window openings transports me to the space where the fresco originally was.

**Figure 8 Fresco  recovered from a recess**

Checking the time, we buy a few items in their gift shop and head out to the formidable steps to find a taxi. Now we appreciate the extra effort our driver took to deliver us to the foot of the last set of stairs to the museum. We look out over the grand stairs and waterfalls that lead from the museum to the city street far, far, far below. Two sets of stairs, which probably do have five hundred steps each, flank three pools of water which cascade from one to the next and end at a broad plaza with a pool extending most of its width, four tall columns, and several spires of water.

**Figure 9 Top half of steps to Museum of Catalonian Art.**

Then it's another hundred or so steps from that plaza to the street, but there is an escalator for this part of the journey.

It's not moving.

I check to see if there is a sensor that turns it on when I approach. No such luck. We go to the stairs and start our descent, legs aching from the stairs already taken. Going down steps always seems harder than going up them.

Part way down, I look up the street and see a taxi at a stand in mid-block. The driver is standing outside apparently looking for riders. This is serendipitous; it looks like I will leave the museum, walk down a thousand stairs, step into a waiting taxi, and drive to the Sagrada Familia just like it happens in the movies. I wave my arms, but the driver gets into the cab and drives away. This is real life, not the movies.

We finally finish descending the interminable stairs and go to the taxi stand to hail a cab. Several pass by, but they either already have passengers or simply ignore us. We seem to be invisible.

Farther down the street, where it meets a large roundabout, people are successfully hailing cabs. We move to the corner and try again. A cab stops, but a lady dashes in front of us and jumps into it before we can even take a step. We seem to be still wearing our invisibility cloaks. Several other people are getting rides, but even when we stand right on the curb and a taxi comes by, it slides past us to the people twenty feet away. We move over to that spot, and now the cabs stop where we were before.

Sandra bravely crosses the street to the opposite corner, mopeds and cars flowing around her like water around a rock in a river. She's awesome. And fits right in with the locals' expectations. After only a minute or so, a cab stops in front of her, and I make the mad dash through traffic to get in. Did the driver stop because he thought it was a single woman he would be picking up? We'll never know, but when I say, "Sagrada Familia, *por favor*," he responds "*Si. Si.*" and we are on our way.

## LA SAGRADA FAMILIA – PART 2

We arrive at Sagrada Familia and, as usual, the sidewalks are full of people. Some are in line to get tickets (which we already know are sold out for today), some are in line waiting to get in, and most are simply crowding around admiring the cathedral. The packed people present a pickpocket's paradise.

A friendly attendant notices us looking a bit bewildered. He checks our tickets' admission date and time, then asks, "Do you want the English audio guides? They're included in the admission. Just be certain to turn them in when you leave." He then takes Sandra to a room and gives her two devices while I keep our place in line. We key in the number of the display we are at, press play, and the device describes what is right in front of us.

We go in through the nativity entrance and find ourselves in another world. A world that somehow seems larger than the one we just left. This world soars into heaven itself. All the architectural lines are vertical, and they are long. The modern multi-story stained-glass windows over the entrance bathe us in cool and calming blue and green light signifying the start of a new day. Looking to the other side of the cathedral we see the fiery red, yellow, and orange hues over the passion entrance, evoking the end of the day — or possibly the end times.

The immediate overall impression is of light and delicacy. The massive columns even seem light and almost fragile. Like trees, each column begins as a stolid trunk that becomes thinner and thinner the higher it soars until it evolves into smaller and thinner branches that finally end at the peak of the nave 148 feet over our heads. We crane our necks to see that high, but risk falling over as we look up. A large table with a mirror for its top sits near the end of the nave opposite the altar, enabling us to look straight up into the towering heavens while looking down. Unlike many other cathedrals, windows bring in light at every level, even near the peak of the nave and each supporting tower. It becomes lighter the higher you look. Heaven shining down upon us.

As with the exterior, symbolism is rampant and overwhelms my ability to absorb it in the moment. I find another magic square with numbers totaling thirty-three. Images in the stained-glass windows illustrate Biblical events. Doves emerge from the smallest branches of the columns. The columns of the four Evangelists are brown instead of grey like the others, and each has a shield with the Evangelist's logo. Standing in the midst of La Sagrada

Familia, the totality of the building makes me feel small but still significant and empowered. I am an essential part of the cosmos.

Leaving by the passion exit, we return our listening devices, catch our breath, return to the normal world, and explore the museum and gift shop under the cathedral. The museum shows pictures of the progress in construction and models of some of the main components that were tested in the workshop to verify structural integrity and develop construction techniques. We buy some tea towels, medallions, and magic square cufflinks and earrings for people on our gift list. Finding a taxi back to our hotel is much easier here since we can simply get in one that is discharging passengers at the church. Once in the taxi, we realize how tired we are from walking and standing. We also realize we are very hungry.

## OUR LAST SUPPER

Just a few steps from the hotel we slip into the Solric Pizza & Grill Restaurant. They have a wonderful selection of salads, a couple of soups, pastas, paellas, meats, fish, burgers, twenty-one pizzas (after all, it is the Solric **Pizza** & Grill Restaurant), calzone, a modest selection of wines, and some wonderful desserts. I am glad they did not have a wine list that goes on for pages and pages. I'd rather take the same time to read a good short story than slog my way through a long wine list. We each have a glass of sangria and start with the *Ensalada Solric* with arugula, mozzarella, avocado, and apple with vinaigrette honey and mustard dressing. Since this is our last night in Spain, I decide to have a traditional Spanish dish as my entrée. The *Paella Marinera* is a delicious and lightly spiced dish of fresh seafood: calamari, fish, scallops, and oysters. Although greatly tempted by the large selection of pizzas, Sandra selects the *Calzone Especial* since calzone rarely appears on menus. She relishes the ham, chicken, mozzarella, veal, pepperoni, and Neapolitan sauce with olive oil and Parmesan cheese sprinkled on top. I top off my meal with the *Flan casero* (homemade flan) and Sandra goes French in Spain with the Profiteroles bathed in chocolate and nuts accompanied by cream. A wonderful meal.

Tired, but now sated, we head to bed and put in a 5:30 a.m. wakeup call for our trip home.

# 8 – HOMEWARD BOUND

After a very quick very early breakfast we are on our way to Barcelona airport for our flight to Atlanta and US Customs. It's a smooth ten-hour flight during which I nap and Sandra refines the course she will be teaching in two weeks. I am relieved we arrive in Atlanta a half-hour early, which gives us a bit more time to get our bags, go through Customs, re-check our bags, and find our flight to Ontario, California.

Once through Customs, we must go to another terminal building because domestic flights, for some reason, always leave from a building at the opposite end of the airport from where Customs is. It doesn't take long to find the tram that swiftly transports us to Terminal B, and we are at our departure gate with an hour and forty-five minutes to spare. I much prefer waiting to dashing madly through the airport hoping the airline knows we are on our way and won't close the plane's door just as we get the gate in sight.

Since we have checked our bags, we don't rush when it comes time to board. Our seats will not be taken by someone boarding before us. We need not stress or push to be the first in our boarding group to get on the plane so we can find an overhead bin near our seats. Our bags all fit under the seat in front of us. My biggest concerns are that a parent with a colicky infant will be in the third seat in our row, or that a rambunctious child in the seat behind one of us will kick and pull on our seat for the entire flight. No colicky infants or rambunctious children on this flight. Hooray!

Four and a half hours later we land, meet our driver, find our bags, and are on the last leg of our trip. We arrive home at mid-evening. It's been a great trip visiting new places, puttering around Florence in a tiny car, shopping for olive oil, surviving another wine tasting, exploring a villa and a château, and being spiritually uplifted by a grand cathedral still under construction. But it's always nice to be home — and we immediately look forward to our next adventure.

Spot's next adventure is

*TRAVELS WITH SPOT:*

*Into the Midnight Sun* coming in 2026.

# I

A year earlier my wife, Sandra, and I took an ocean cruise from Rome to Barcelona in late July, celebrating our 50th wedding anniversary in Barcelona. Wonderful cities, but too hot in late July (over 100 degrees Fahrenheit in Florence), so we signed up for what we hoped would be a cooler August Viking Ocean cruise: "Into the Midnight Sun" starting in London and ending in Bergen, Norway.

## GETTING THERE IS HALF THE FUN (?)

We arrive at the United Airlines counter at Ontario, California, International Airport three hours before the scheduled 10:56 a.m. departure time to check our bags. There are six other people in line, but there is no one behind the counter. The instructions on the reservations are very clear: arrive at the airport at least three hours before the start of an international flight. We are there, but no one from the airline is. We wait. And we wait. After 45 minutes, I search for someone to find out why there is no one at the counter. A TSA agent says they have nothing to do with the airlines. An airport security guard says they have nothing to do with the airlines. A janitor says the airlines don't send anyone to their counters until about an hour before the flight time. Never underestimate the knowledge of the janitor. We now have another hour and a quarter to wait for an agent to show up at the counter. The line gets longer and longer and more and more restless. I pass along my message from the janitor, and the line calms down—a bit.

A big agent, possibly from Samoa, finally arrives. As he passes the line he says, "You could have checked in with the kiosks."

"But we have bags to check," several people reply.

"The kiosks can print baggage tags," he retorts.

"And where would we put the bags?"

"Leave them at the counter, and we would get them."

Really? Just leave the bags at the counter?

Just then the general announcement comes over the loudspeakers, "Do not leave bags or parcels unattended. Report any unattended bags or parcels to security. Unattended items are subject to confiscation."

The agent finally goes behind the counter, taking several minutes to start the computers and get set up before motioning to the people first in line. Once he gets going, he is quite efficient, checking reservations, issuing boarding passes, and tagging and moving bags to the conveyor belt behind him.

He is surprised that Sandra and I are checking our bags since they are apparently small enough to go as carry-on luggage. I explain, "We don't want to drag the bags through the airports and then try swinging them up into an overhead bin. Besides, Sandra can't reach the overhead bins. Please just check them through to London."

He tags the bags somewhat reluctantly, gives us the claim stubs, and we head toward the security checkpoint.

TSA is the usual scene of agents talking with each other, largely ignoring the passengers. One occasionally yells out, "Put everything in the bins. Computers out of their cases. No liquids over 3 ounces. Wait for an agent to wave you into the scanner." Happily, there is one gentle agent helping people get bins and separate their items so bins are not overloaded. Computers, of course, have to be in their own bins.

"Do I need to take off my shoes?" I ask.

"Are you over 75?"

"In 40 days."

"Shoes and belt in a bin, then." Perhaps I should have lied, but I don't want to risk raising the ire of the TSA if they check my ID and then decide I must be hiding something and give me a strip search. Sandra, being over 75, sails right through security while I struggle to untie my shoes, remove my belt, and find yet another bin.

Holding my pants up with one hand, I wait for an agent to wave me into the full body scanner. As I step in and raise both hands over my head, I hope my pants will stay up. They do, as long as I keep my feet far apart.

I find my bins and ponder the necessity of men removing their belts. Most men need belts to keep their pants in place, while many women's belts are more accessories. Removing my belt seems like a hazing ritual: something embarrassing act required to join the group—in this case, those going to a plane. I've never seen them ask someone to remove their suspenders, which often have as much metal in their clips as a belt has in its buckle. Maybe I should wear suspenders the next time.

When I get to my bins, which have somehow gotten separated from each other even though they started out together, there is considerable peer pressure to just grab my stuff and get going. As I collect my things, I recall a presentation by a TSA official who showed us large bags of things people had left at only one security checkpoint in the last three months: over sixty cell phones, car and house keys, a few laptops, and even a few pairs of shoes. He told us that if we were travelling and lost something, contact the TSA and they will review the video from the time you were at the checkpoint; if they have your item, they will hold it for you to pick up at the end of your trip.

My first task is finding my belt and putting it on so I can use both hands. Then I put the computer back into its case, slip into my shoes, hobble away to a bench where I finish putting my belongings together (Why is my watch in a different bin than I put it in?), tie my shoes, and leave to find my wife who passed inspection without a hitch and we jointly search for the gate.

The last of the stores are opening for business as the airport finishes waking up while we walk to the departure lounge. That name, "departure lounge," conjures images of comfortable overstuffed leather chairs, possibly some La-Z-Boy or Barcalounger recliners, and a bar at one side with staff stopping by asking if you would like a drink or a newspaper or magazine, and with soft calming music in the background or even a pianist playing vaguely familiar and highly embellished tunes on a grand piano. In fact, it's rows of bench-seats bolted to the floor with an occasional electrical outlet in the vicinity of the exit ramp to the airplane, and occasional, largely unintelligible, announcements made hurriedly on the general speaker system.

The plane pulls into place at about 10:15. Our flight is scheduled to begin boarding at 10:20 and depart at 10:56. At 10:50 they announce the flight is be delayed because of a "mechanical issue." While it is comforting to know they will not let us on the plane until it is fully functional, it is a bit disturbing that I saw the plane land only thirty-five minutes earlier and now there is a mechanical issue that keeps it from flying.

We start boarding at 11:25, push back from the gate at 11:50, and are on our way to San Francisco-Oakland Airport for our flight to London. The trip to SFO is largely uneventful with sunny skies and nice views of California mountains, the San Joaquin Valley, and San Francisco Bay before landing at 12:37. There is plenty of time to find our gate and get lunch before the next leg of our journey to London Heathrow Airport (LHR) which is scheduled to leave at 4:00 p.m. It is quite a long walk, because, of course, the domestic flights use a whole different wing of the terminal than the international flights. Twenty minutes or so later we find our gate's departure lounge and scout the eateries and restrooms in the vicinity. Sandra and I share a soup and sandwich at a shop just outside and above the gate to our flight. I watch a young boy, perhaps seven or eight, go down and then up the stairs, down and up. He does this perhaps ten times as his older sister looks on. Children that age often simply must run or climb stairs before they become totally exhausted and then fall fast asleep. It's quite fun to watch—when it's not your child.

After eating, we go down to the departure area and Sandra finds a seat with an outlet to plug in her computer. She goes to work writing the memoir of a friend and reviewing materials for a graduate research methods class she would begin teaching soon after we return. I watch the people. There are many nationalities and several languages. Single travelers find places apart from the others, clearly not wanting to engage, turning their backs to the crowd. There are a few couples who are oblivious to the crowds around them. Newlyweds? Lovers? The remainder are families of all sizes, some with small children and babies, others with teenagers and adult children and grandparents. Parts of the families wander off only to be rounded up by other members. Jackets and backpacks taken off and dropped on the floor are later retrieved by parents or siblings. A few people, most apparently Americans, spend their time staring at their smartphones and typing messages or playing Candy Crush or some other video game.

Scheduled boarding time comes and goes without comment or announcement. At about 4:30, a half hour after we were supposed to depart, boarding starts. Once we are all aboard, bags stowed, and seated, they announce that the flight is delayed because of a "mechanical issue with one of the engines." I look out the window and see a bunch of workers roll a scaffold up to the right engine, open the cowling, and start digging around inside. After an hour or so they announce that the problem is "a sticky valve which they should fix in a few minutes."

Moments later, they announce, "Those who want, can get off the plane and go into the terminal if you want. If you deplane you must scan your boarding pass on the way out and will have to scan it again when you re-board the plane."

Sandra and I decide to just stay on the plane.

At 6:48 they button up the engine (close the cowling which provides a smooth path for the air past the engine) and people start re-boarding. At 7:25 we push away from the terminal and are on our way—three hours and twenty-five minutes late. Happily, we have eight hours between our originally scheduled arrival time and the earliest time we could board the ship in London, so we remain relaxed (as long as the sticky valve works properly). While the seat-back entertainment systems are certainly a boon, an hour after takeoff I pull out my sleep mask, put it on, and get some rest.

We were originally due to arrive at 06:25 the next morning. We actually arrive at Heathrow at 06:38 even though we departed nearly three and a half hours late. The pilot must have caught a very strong tail wind and really revved the engines. Well done!

The walk from the plane to baggage claim............

To be continued.

www.ingramcontent.com/pod-product-compliance
Lightning Source LLC
Chambersburg PA
CBHW071534120626
46550CB00006B/2449